HUE COLORING

50 LOVELY HORSE DESIGNS
An Adult Coloring Book

ISBN-13: 978-1530442492
ISBN-10: 1530442494

IN THIS COLORING BOOK...

50 Lovely Horse Designs are included in this adult coloring book to help you relax and make your life more colorful. These illustrations are created for you to bring enjoyment to life, and designed with beautiful patterns that appeal to adult eyes.

TIPS TO A FUN COLORING

Find a quiet space. It's easier to focus on what you are doing when there are no distractions.

Organize your materials. Lay out your coloring book and crayons, pens, or pencils.

Set the mood. Turn on some tranquil music, diffuse lavender or another relaxing oil, and make sure you have your preferred drink at hand.

Select your picture. Which image speaks to you today? That's the one you should color. Choose your palette. Select the colors you will be using for your image.

Begin coloring. This is the fun part. Don't worry about getting everything perfect; just start. If you feel you don't want to do it anymore, just stop!

SHOW US YOUR CREATION!

We'd love to hear from you, show us what you created.
Facebook: www.facebook.com/huecoloring
Pinterest: www.pinterest.com/huecoloring

Please be sure to subscribe to our newsletter by visiting: huecoloring.com. We'll show you our latest coloring projects as well as giving you information of the best deals.

SHOW US YOUR CREATION!

We'd love to hear from you, show us what you created.
Facebook: www.facebook.com/huecoloring
Pinterest: www.pinterest.com/huecoloring

Please be sure to subscribe to our newsletter by visiting:
huecoloring.com. We'll show you our latest coloring projects as
well as giving you information of the best deals.